SCIENCE FOR THE FUTURE

BRAIN–COMPUTER INTERFACES

by Lisa J. Amstutz

www.focusreaders.com

Copyright © 2020 by Focus Readers, Lake Elmo, MN 55042. All rights reserved. No part of this book may be reproduced or utilized in any form or by any means without written permission from the publisher.

Focus Readers is distributed by North Star Editions:
sales@northstareditions.com | 888-417-0195

Produced for Focus Readers by Red Line Editorial.

Content Consultant: Dr. Dennis Barbour, Department of Biomedical Engineering, Washington University in St. Louis

Photographs ©: Niall Carson/PA Wire URN:37735303/AP Images, cover, 1; BSIP/Newscom, 4–5, 24; EThamPhoto/Alamy, 7; Apic/Retired/Hulton Archive/Getty Images, 8–9; Chaikom/Shutterstock Images, 10; F. Astier/Centre Hospitalier Régional Universitaire de Lille/Science Source, 13; Sebastian Kaulitzki/Shutterstock Images, 14–15; BlueRingMedia/Shutterstock Images, 17; Red Line Editorial, 19; Jared Siskin/Patrick McMullan/Getty Images, 21; Craig F. Walker/The Boston Globe/Getty Images, 22–23; Pau Barrena/AFP/Getty Images, 27; Susan Walsh/AP Images, 29; Tammy Ljungblad/The Kansas City Star/AP Images, 30–31; Alistair Heap/Alamy, 33; Kathy Hutchins/Shutterstock Images, 35; Dr P. Marazzi/Science Source, 36–37; Joe McNally/Hulton Archive/Getty Images, 39; FunKey Factory/Shutterstock Images, 41; Teeradej/Shutterstock Images, 42–43; Volker Steger/Science Source, 45

Library of Congress Cataloging-in-Publication Data
Names: Amstutz, Lisa J., author.
Title: Brain-computer interfaces / by Lisa J. Amstutz.
Description: Lake Elmo, MN : Focus Readers, [2020] | Series: Science for the future | Audience: Grades 7 to 8. | Includes bibliographical references and index.
Identifiers: LCCN 2019008553 (print) | LCCN 2019010193 (ebook) | ISBN 9781644930014 (pdf) | ISBN 9781641859158 (ebook) | ISBN 9781641857772 (hardcover) | ISBN 9781641858465 (pbk.).
Subjects: LCSH: Brain-computer interfaces--Juvenile literature. | Biomedical engineering--Juvenile literature. | Neuroprostheses--Juvenile literature. | Human-computer interaction--Juvenile literature.
Classification: LCC QA76.9.H85 (ebook) | LCC QA76.9.H85 A57 2020 (print) | DDC 610.28--dc23
LC record available at https://lccn.loc.gov/2019008553

Printed in the United States of America
Mankato, MN
May, 2019

ABOUT THE AUTHOR

Lisa J. Amstutz is the author of more than 100 children's books. She specializes in topics related to science and agriculture. Lisa's background includes degrees in biology and environmental science. When she's not writing, you may find her walking in the woods or enjoying a cup of tea and a good book.

TABLE OF CONTENTS

CHAPTER 1
Brain Games 5

CHAPTER 2
The History of BCIs 9

CHAPTER 3
How BCIs Work 15

SCIENTIST BIO
Helen Mayberg 20

CHAPTER 4
Helping People Move 23

SCIENTIST BIO
Andrew Schwartz 28

CHAPTER 5
Making Connections 31

CHAPTER 6
Challenges Ahead 37

CHAPTER 7
The Future of BCIs 43

Focus on Brain-Computer Interfaces • 46
Glossary • 47
To Learn More • 48
Index • 48

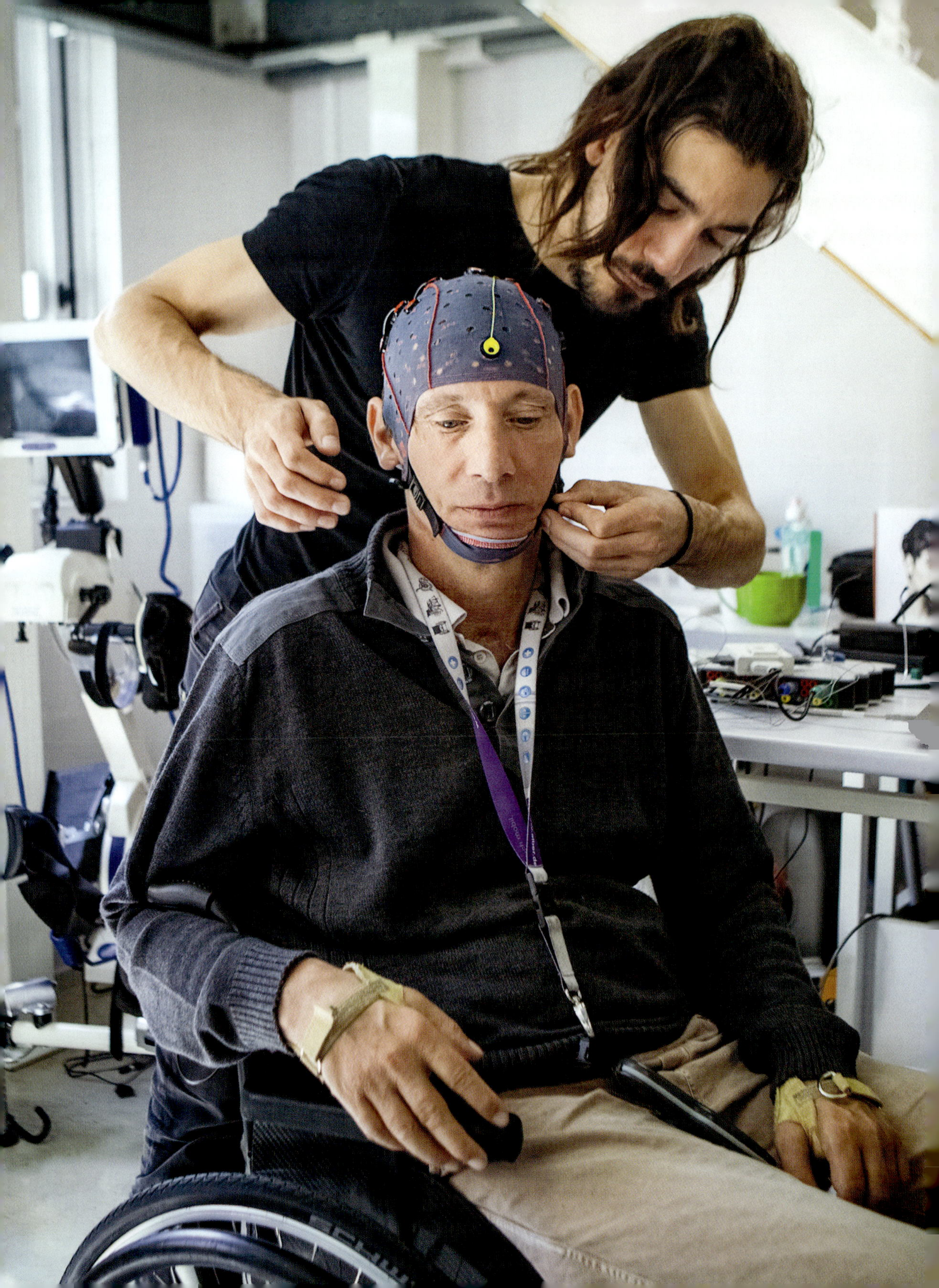

CHAPTER 1

BRAIN GAMES

The racers lined up and focused their minds. Then they were off! They sped down the track and leaped over hurdles. Thanks to technology called a brain-computer interface (BCI), they did all this without moving a muscle. The racers used their thoughts to move characters on a screen.

The race was part of the Cybathlon in 2016. The event was the world's first **bionic** competition. Athletes used BCIs and other new technology.

A man practices using a brain-computer interface so he can race in the Cybathlon.

The human brain contains billions of neurons. These nerve cells connect together end to end. They send messages using chemicals and electricity. When a part of the brain is active, it gives off electrical signals.

A BCI is a connection between a human brain and a device inside or outside the body. Some types of BCIs put electrical signals into the brain. These devices can be used to help with hearing loss, **seizures**, and other conditions.

Other BCIs use sensors to pick up signals from a person's brain. They send these signals to a computer. The computer uses the signals to control a device. The racers used this second type of BCI. Each racer wore a cap covered in **electrodes**. The electrodes sent signals from the racer's brain to a computer. The computer used the signals to determine how the racers wanted

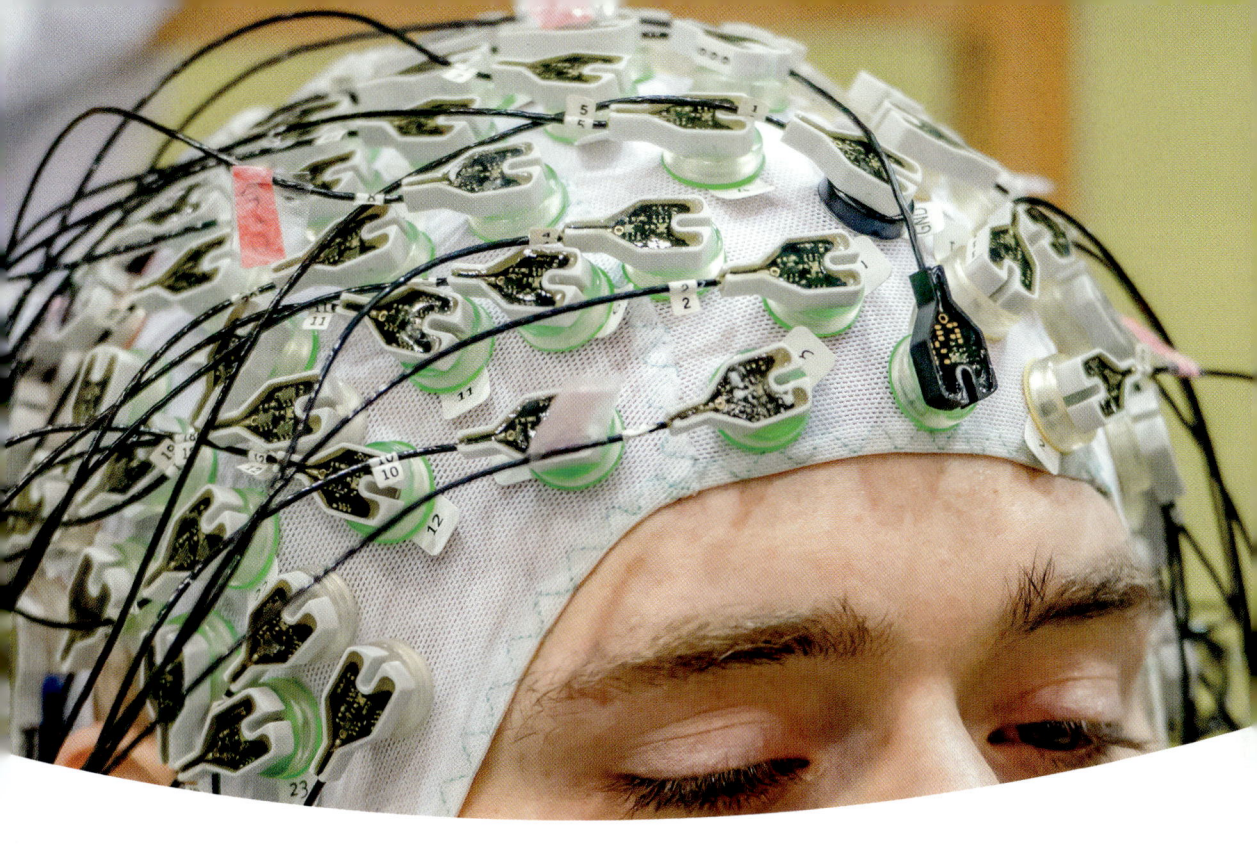

▲ Electrodes send signals from the brain to a computer. The computer then reacts to the person's thoughts.

their characters to move. It told the device how to respond. Racers could make the characters rotate, jump, and slide.

Many other kinds of BCIs are still being tested. These BCIs could help people move or communicate. They could even restore lost senses, such as touch or sight.

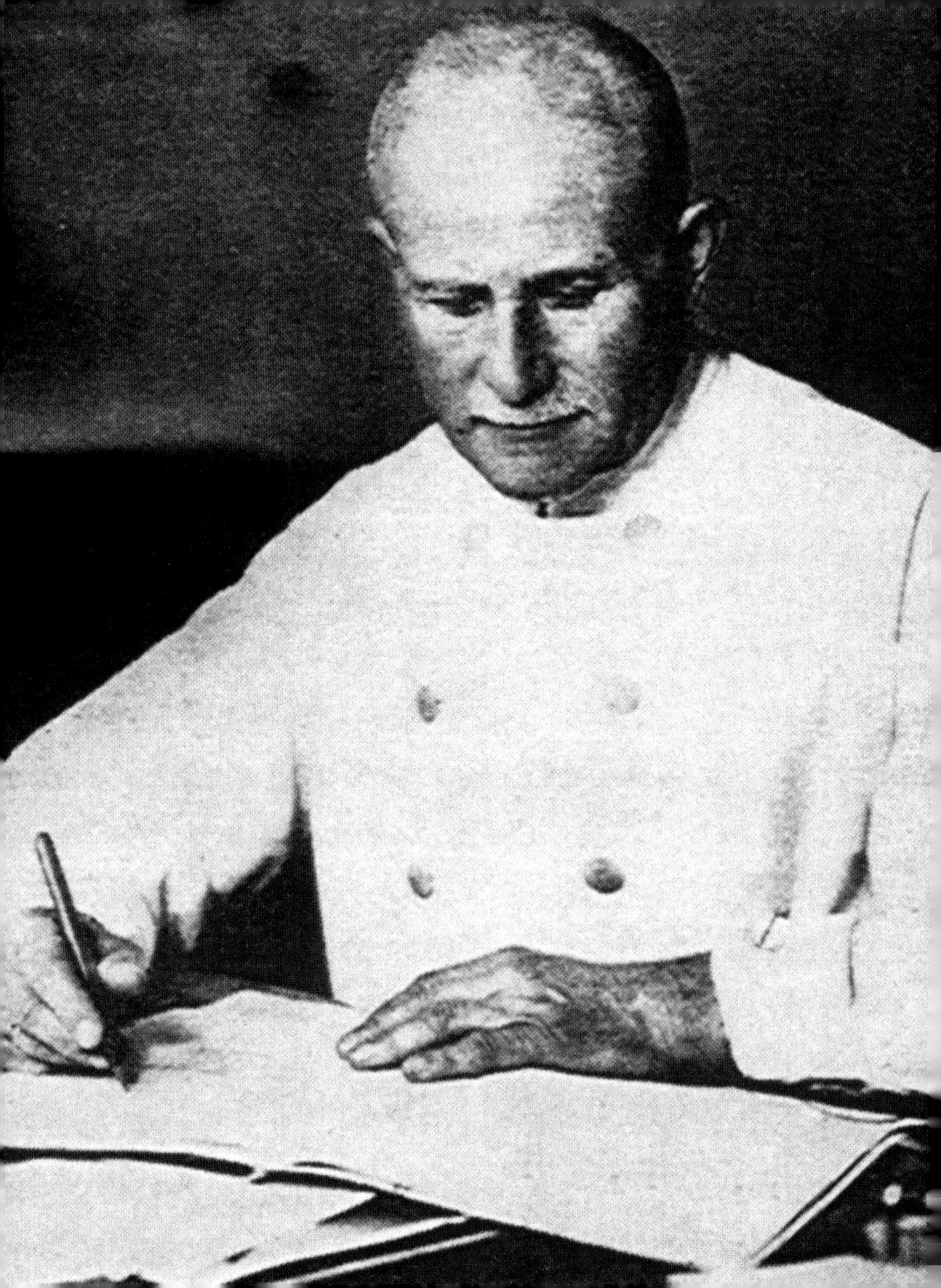

CHAPTER 2

THE HISTORY OF BCIs

The technology behind BCIs took decades to develop. First, scientists had to learn about how signals traveled in the brain. In the 1920s, a scientist named Hans Berger found a way to measure the brain's electrical signals. Berger placed electrodes on a person's scalp. The electrode readings showed which parts of the brain were active. Berger's findings led to the development of the electroencephalogram (EEG).

Hans Berger was a German scientist who discovered a way to record brain signals.

▲ EEGs are still used today to measure brain activity.

This test shows the levels of activity in different parts of a person's brain.

Scientists wanted to see if brain signals could be used to control devices. So, they began tests with monkeys in the 1960s. They attached an electrode to a neuron in each monkey's brain. They connected this electrode to a meter. The meter's needle moved each time the neuron sent a signal. With food as a reward, the monkeys learned to control the needle's movement.

Scientists wanted to try similar tests on humans. But they faced several challenges. Early computers were slow and not very powerful. And scientists had much to learn about how the brain worked. Even so, they made progress.

In the 1970s, a scientist named Jacques Vidal created a BCI that let users move through a maze on a computer screen. Users looked at different parts of a checkerboard. Depending on where they looked, the computer knew to move up, down, left, or right. And in 1972, people began using cochlear **implants**. This type of BCI helps people with hearing loss detect sounds.

In 1988, scientists created a BCI based on P3 signals. These signals appear in the brain shortly after a person notices something of interest.

The BCI flashed letters on a screen. P3 signals appeared when users saw the letter they wanted. The machine selected that letter. It helped users spell words.

Another BCI used sensorimotor rhythms. These brain signals show up when someone moves or thinks about moving. The BCI moved a cursor on a screen when users thought about moving.

For these first BCIs, the electrodes attached to the user's scalp. But in 1996, scientists placed electrodes directly on a human brain. The BCI allowed the patient to choose between two options, like answering a true-or-false question.

➢ THINK ABOUT IT

Sometimes scientists use animals to test difficult or dangerous procedures. Do you think animal testing should be allowed? Why or why not?

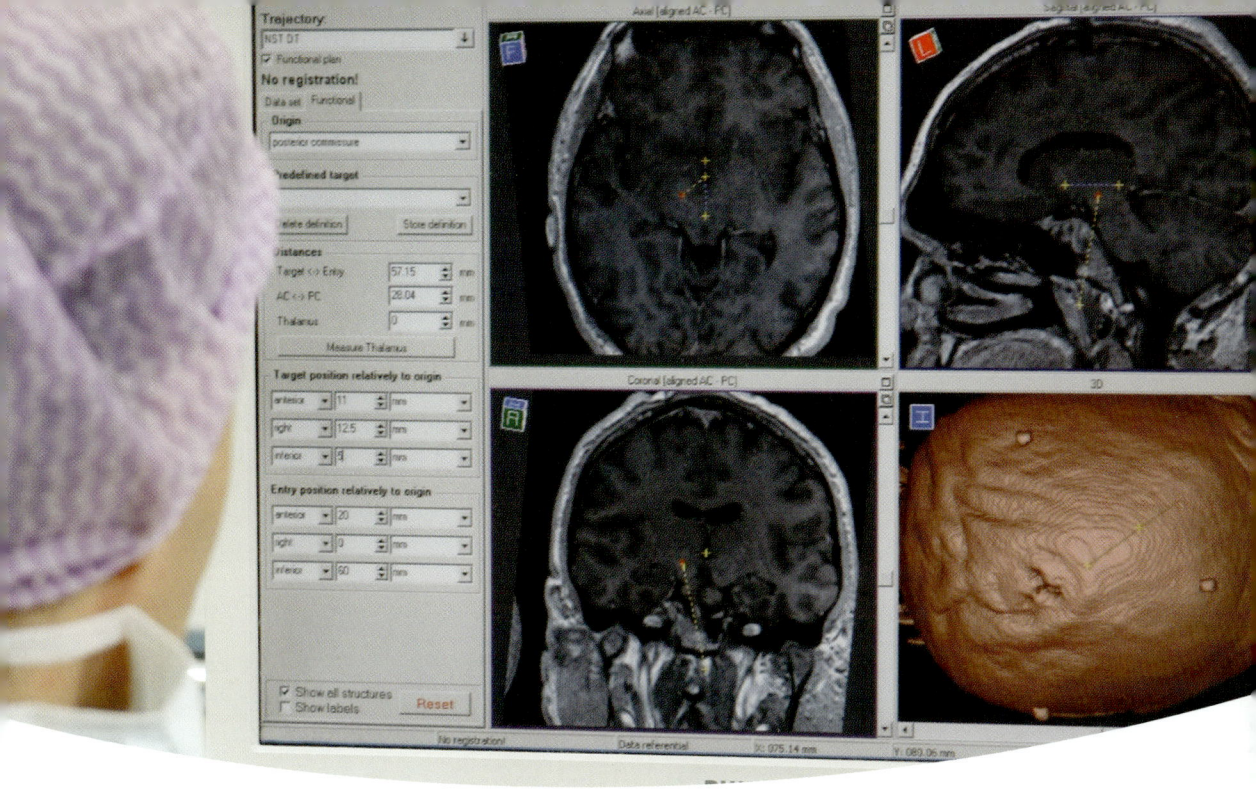

▲ A surgeon views images taken after electrodes were used to treat a patient with Parkinson's.

In 1998, another patient used the BCI to choose letters on a keyboard.

In 2002, another kind of BCI was approved to treat Parkinson's disease. This disease causes shaking movements called tremors. Soon after, scientists began using monkeys to test BCIs that could move a robotic arm. By 2012, they had successfully tested these devices in humans.

13

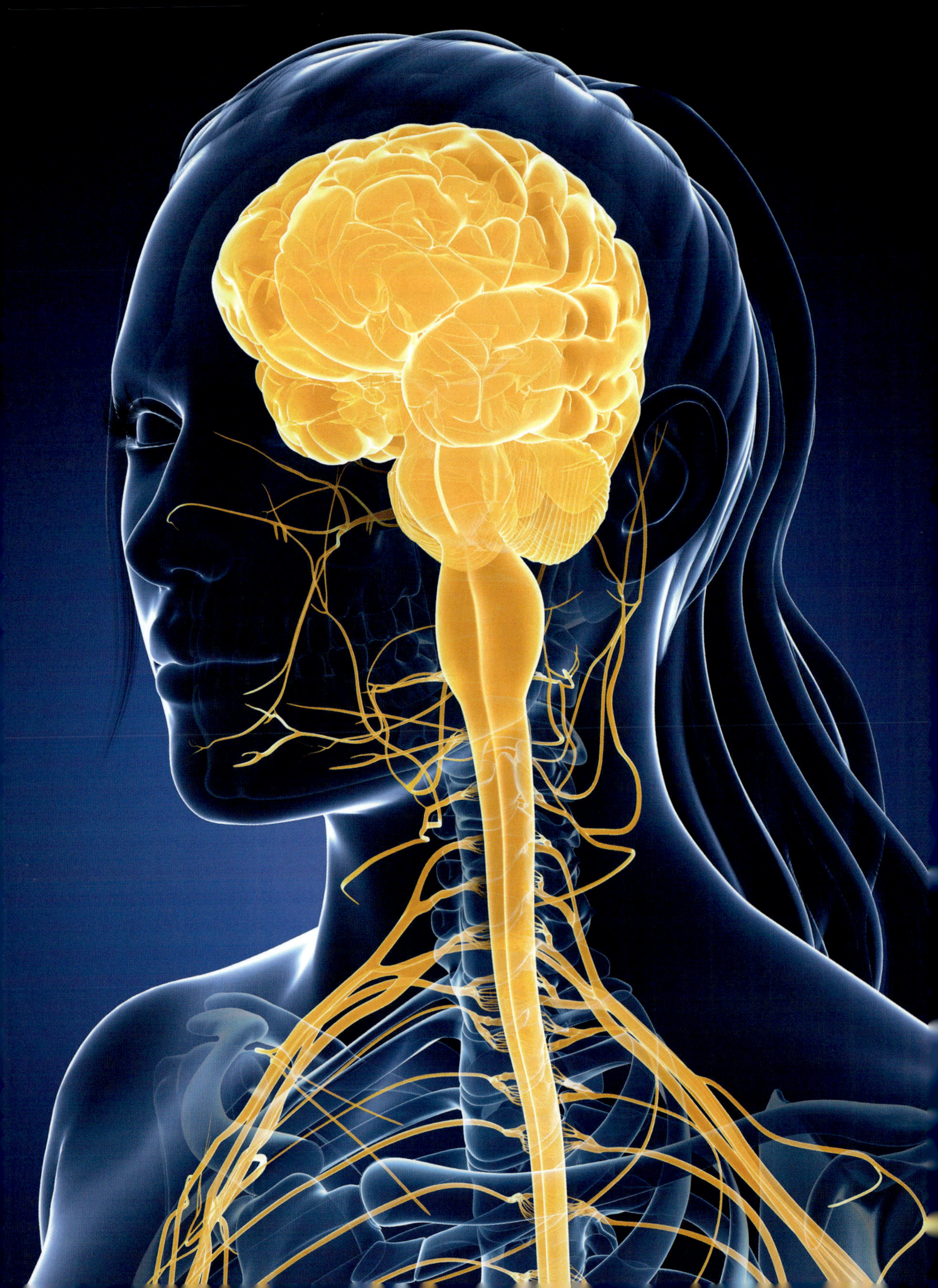

CHAPTER 3

HOW BCIs WORK

All BCIs interact with the user's central nervous system. In humans, this system is made up of the brain and spinal cord. It tells the body how to respond to the outside world and to conditions within the body. It often uses neurons to send signals to the body's cells. The signals tell the cells what to do. They can tell muscles to contract or **glands** to release chemicals. Other neurons send signals back to the central nervous system.

A person's nervous system contains billions and billions of neurons.

For example, the optic nerves send information from the eyes to the brain.

BCIs detect signals from the central nervous system. They send the signals to a computer. Many BCIs use electrodes to measure brain activity. The human brain is made up of several sections. Each section helps with different senses and processes. The brain stem controls basic functions, such as breathing and heartbeat. The cerebellum helps with movement. The cerebrum is responsible for more complex thinking. It is made up of several sections called lobes. Each lobe specializes in certain tasks.

In some BCI systems, the electrodes attach to the person's scalp. They are often held in place by a cap. An EEG reads their signals. The electrodes can gather signals from many parts of the brain. But the person's skull blocks some of the signals.

In other systems, sensors go inside a person's skull. They are placed on the surface of the brain or in the brain's outer layer. These sensors are much more accurate than scalp sensors. They are also riskier. Placing them requires surgery.

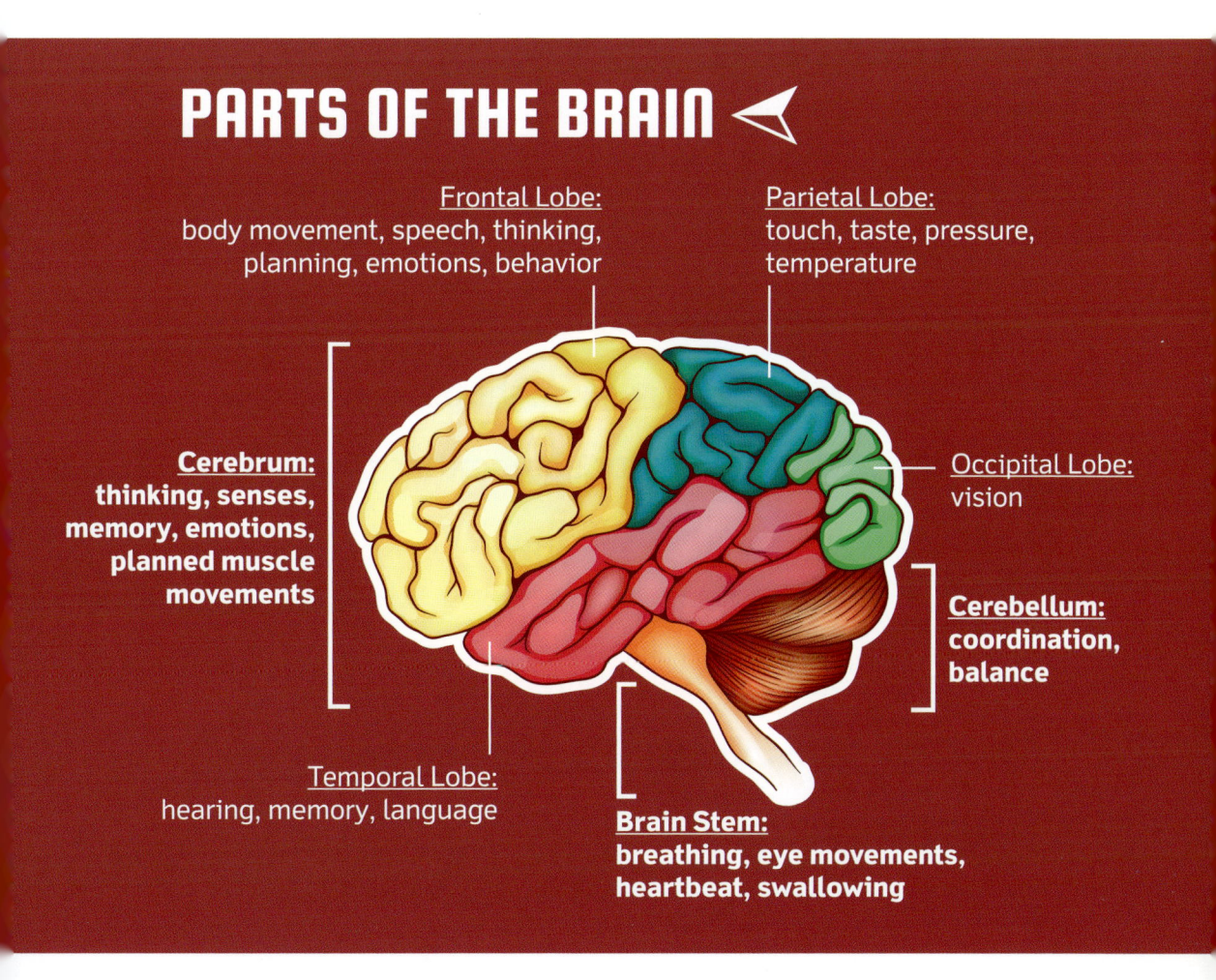

PARTS OF THE BRAIN

Frontal Lobe: body movement, speech, thinking, planning, emotions, behavior

Parietal Lobe: touch, taste, pressure, temperature

Cerebrum: thinking, senses, memory, emotions, planned muscle movements

Occipital Lobe: vision

Cerebellum: coordination, balance

Temporal Lobe: hearing, memory, language

Brain Stem: breathing, eye movements, heartbeat, swallowing

Surgeons must be careful not to damage delicate brain tissue.

Most sensors used in BCIs collect electrical signals. Some can pick up magnetic or **metabolic** signals as well. The signals are sent from the brain to an amplifier. The amplifier makes the signals clearer. Then the signals go to a converter. It turns them into digital signals that a computer can read.

Next, the signals are sent to a device that can complete a specific task. It might be a computer program, a robotic arm, or some other piece of equipment. The signals tell the device to perform some kind of action. For example, scientists are testing a BCI that would help paralyzed people move their arms. To use it, a person thinks about moving an arm. Electrodes pick up signals from the person's motor cortex. This part of the brain controls movement. The electrodes send the signals to a computer, which reads and amplifies them. Then the BCI triggers a set of electrodes in the user's arm. The electrodes stimulate the arm muscles. That causes the person's arm to move.

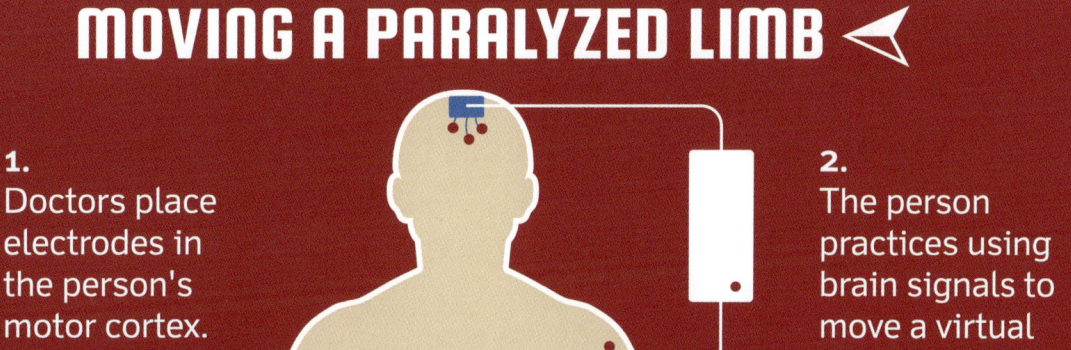

MOVING A PARALYZED LIMB

1. Doctors place electrodes in the person's motor cortex.

2. The person practices using brain signals to move a virtual arm.

3. Doctors place electrodes in the person's arm muscles.

4. When the user thinks about moving, the BCI signals the electrodes in the arm. These electrodes cause the arm to move.

SCIENTIST BIO

HELEN MAYBERG

Dr. Helen Mayberg is a scientist who studies deep brain stimulation (DBS). This type of BCI uses electrodes placed deep in the brain. It sends signals that disrupt the activity between brain regions. In 2002, the FDA approved DBS as a treatment for Parkinson's disease. Doctors can use electrodes to send pulses to the parts of the brain that control movement. This helps lessen the disease's symptoms.

Dr. Mayberg thought DBS could help patients with other conditions. Her research focused on severe depression. Mayberg mapped the parts of the brain involved in depression. She identified an area of the brain called Brodmann area 25, or BA25. This area is connected to parts of the brain that affect emotion, memory, sleep, and more. Deep sadness activates BA25 and shuts down some of these functions in the brain.

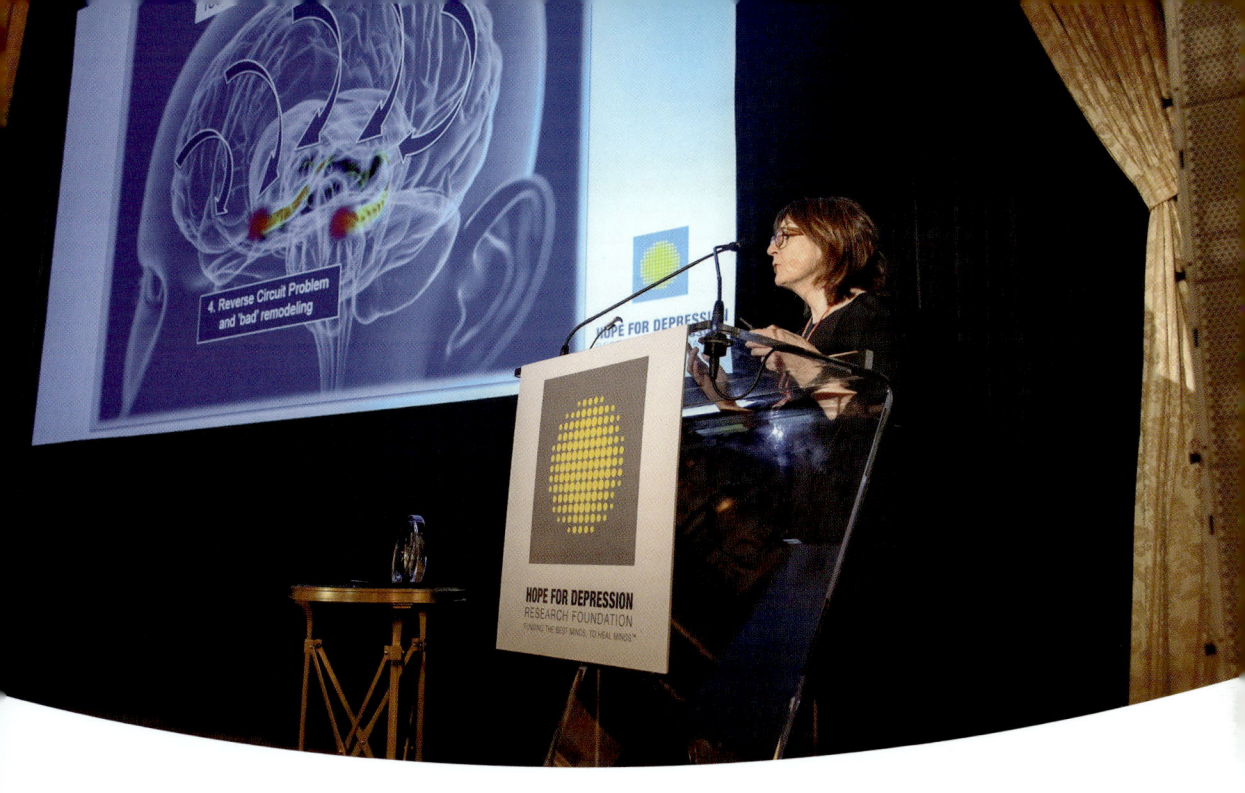

▲ Dr. Helen Mayberg is a leader in deep brain stimulation research.

In the early 2000s, Mayberg's team began testing DBS for patients with severe depression. They used it to disrupt signals in the BA25 area of the patients' brains.

As of 2018, the FDA had not yet approved the use of DBS for depression. But Mayberg continues to lead research in this field. And DBS has been approved for other conditions, including epilepsy and obsessive-compulsive disorder (OCD).

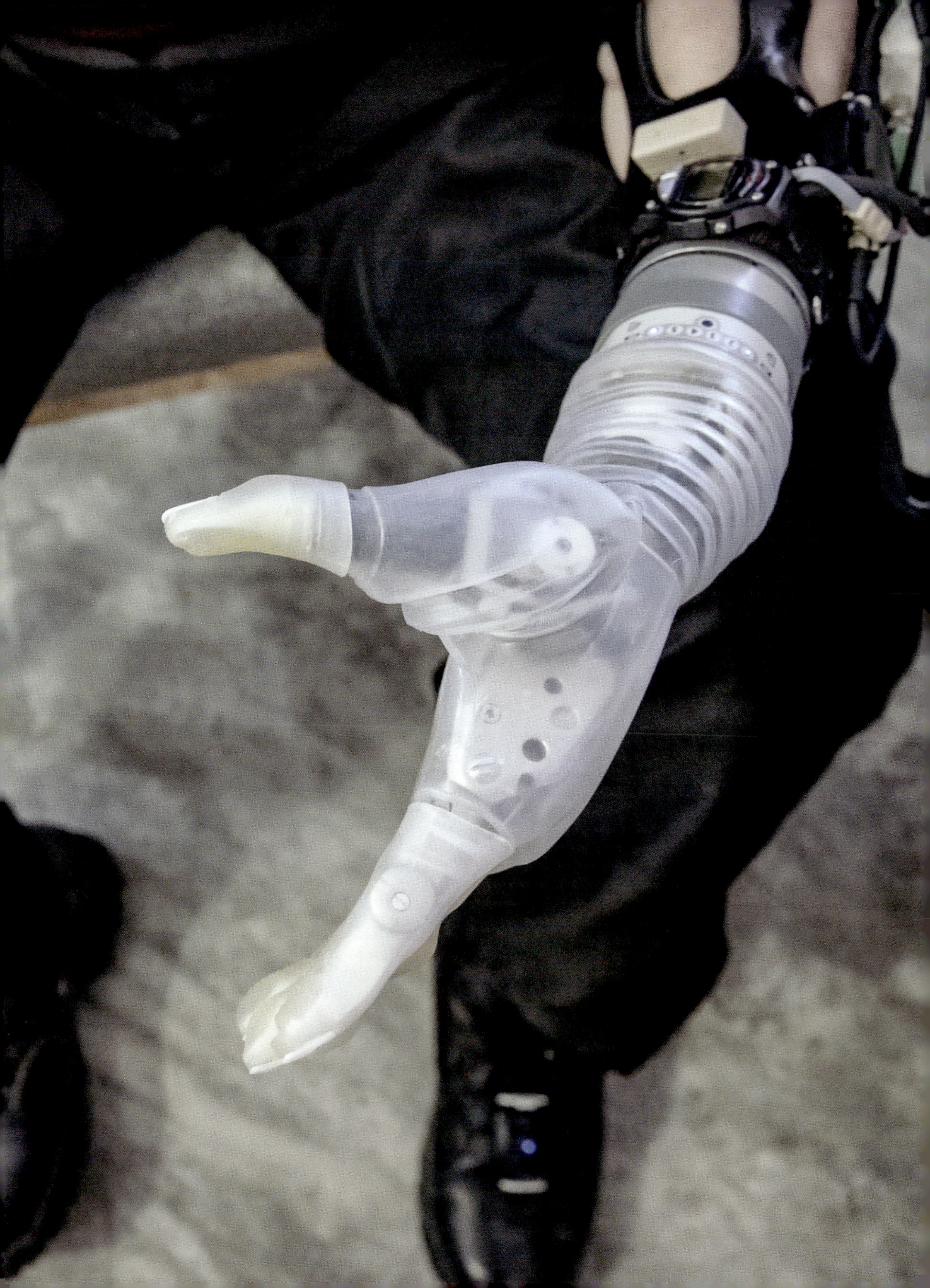

CHAPTER 4

HELPING PEOPLE MOVE

BCIs have great potential to help people who cannot move their limbs. Some BCIs could control wheelchairs or move **prosthetic** limbs. Other BCIs could adjust a room's lighting or control a television.

To operate a BCI device, users must control their brain activity. Most people do not know how to do this. Tests have shown that this skill can be learned. However, it requires practice.

BCIs could help people control prosthetic limbs.

▲ A man practices using a BCI that helps him move his paralyzed legs.

People must train to control their brain signals. They often use a video game–style program. Tasks gradually get harder as the person improves.

In a 2012 study, a woman who was paralyzed from the neck down learned to move a robotic arm and hand. Her BCI used a sheet of electrodes made up of 96 points. Each point went into her brain. Doctors placed the sheet in her left motor cortex. This part of the brain controls the right arm and hand. After 13 weeks of training, the woman could use brain signals to control the robotic hand. She learned to reach and grasp objects. At the end of the study, she used the arm to pick up a chocolate bar and eat it.

Another study helped a man move his own arm. The man had become paralyzed in a bicycle accident. Doctors placed sensors in the part of his brain related to hand movement. The man trained for four months. Then doctors implanted 36 electrodes in his arm. When the man thought about what he wanted to do, the BCI triggered the electrodes in his arm. These electrodes made his muscles move. Using the BCI, the man could hold a cup of coffee and use a fork.

BCIs can also help patients move by using an exoskeleton. This robotic suit can move a person's limbs. In a 2015 study, scientists in South Korea and Germany created an exoskeleton for the lower limbs. Users wore a cap covered with electrodes. They focused their attention on one of five lights. An EEG showed which light the user focused on. In response, the BCI told the suit how to move. Users could make it sit or stand. They could also move forward, left, or right.

Stimulating a person's muscles, nerves, or spinal cord with electricity can cause them to move. Someday, BCI devices may help people regain their ability to move paralyzed limbs. Systems for grasping, standing, and walking are already being tested. This method could even help paralyzed people control their bladders and bowel movements. A 2016 study followed eight

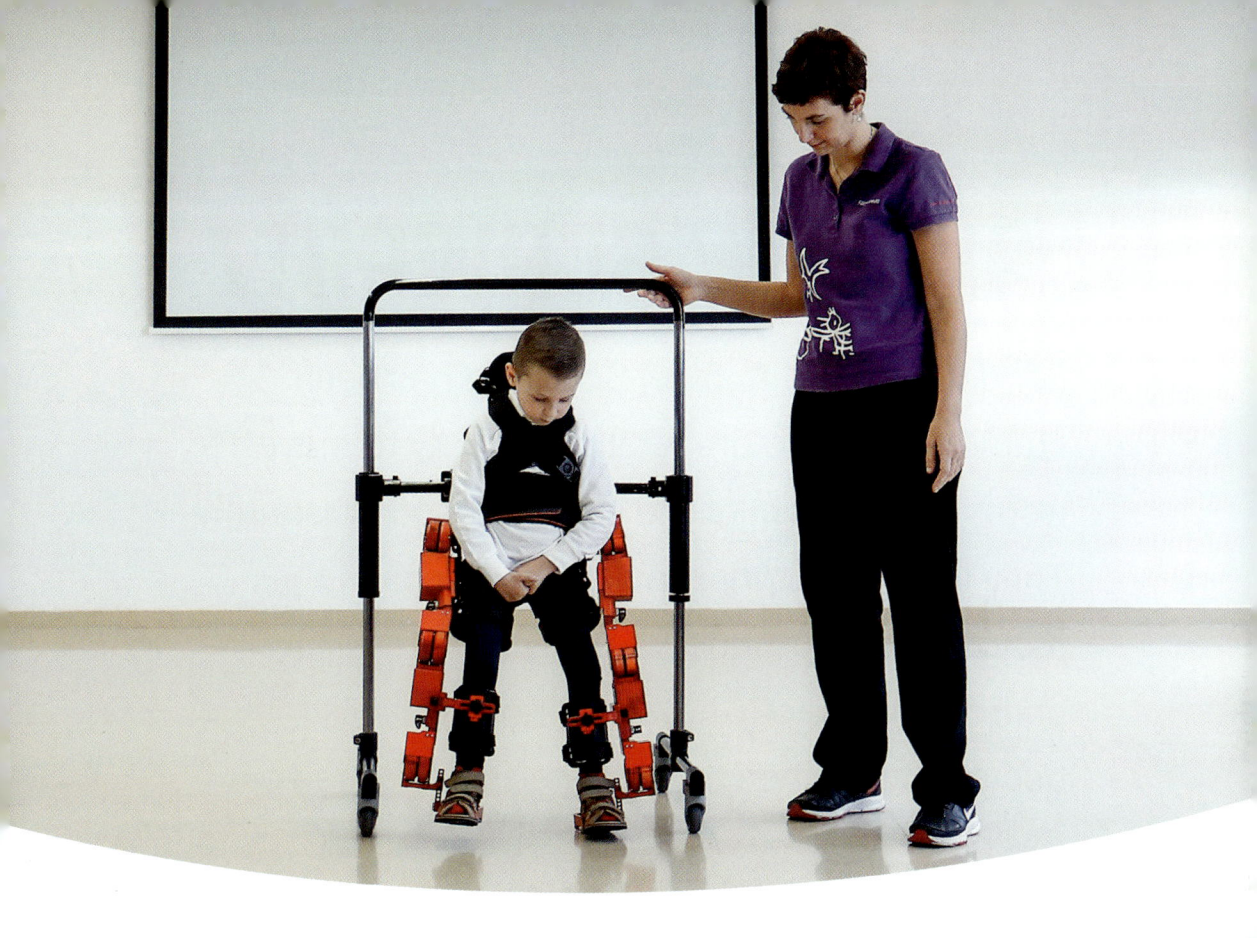

▲ A boy uses an exoskeleton to walk.

people with spinal cord injuries. Their injuries had caused them to become paralyzed in their lower body. After training with BCIs, all eight people partly regained control of their legs. The training also helped with their bowel and bladder control, making them less likely to get infections.

SCIENTIST BIO

ANDREW SCHWARTZ

For decades, Dr. Andrew Schwartz has been studying how the brain tells the body to move. He works with a team at the University of Pittsburgh. They used electrodes to study neurons in the motor cortex of monkeys. They worked to understand exactly how the brain controls the body's limbs. Then they created BCIs based on this data.

Schwartz and his team designed a BCI to control a robotic arm. Starting in the 1990s, they did many tests with monkeys. At first, when a monkey moved its arm, the robotic arm copied its actions. In later tests, monkeys learned to use the arm to feed themselves marshmallows.

In 2011, the team began the first **human trial**. A volunteer had electrodes placed on his brain. He had been paralyzed for several years. But when he thought about moving, the robotic arm

▲ Nathan Copeland (right) used the robotic arm created by Dr. Schwartz to sense touch.

responded. The next year, a woman tested the BCI. She could even control the arm's fingers.

Next, Schwartz and his team worked to add a sense of touch. In 2014, they connected a BCI to the sensory cortex of a man's brain, as well as his motor cortex. When something touched the arm, the man felt it on his own hand.

Dr. Schwartz has received many awards for his pioneering work with BCIs. He continues to push the boundaries of what this technology can do.

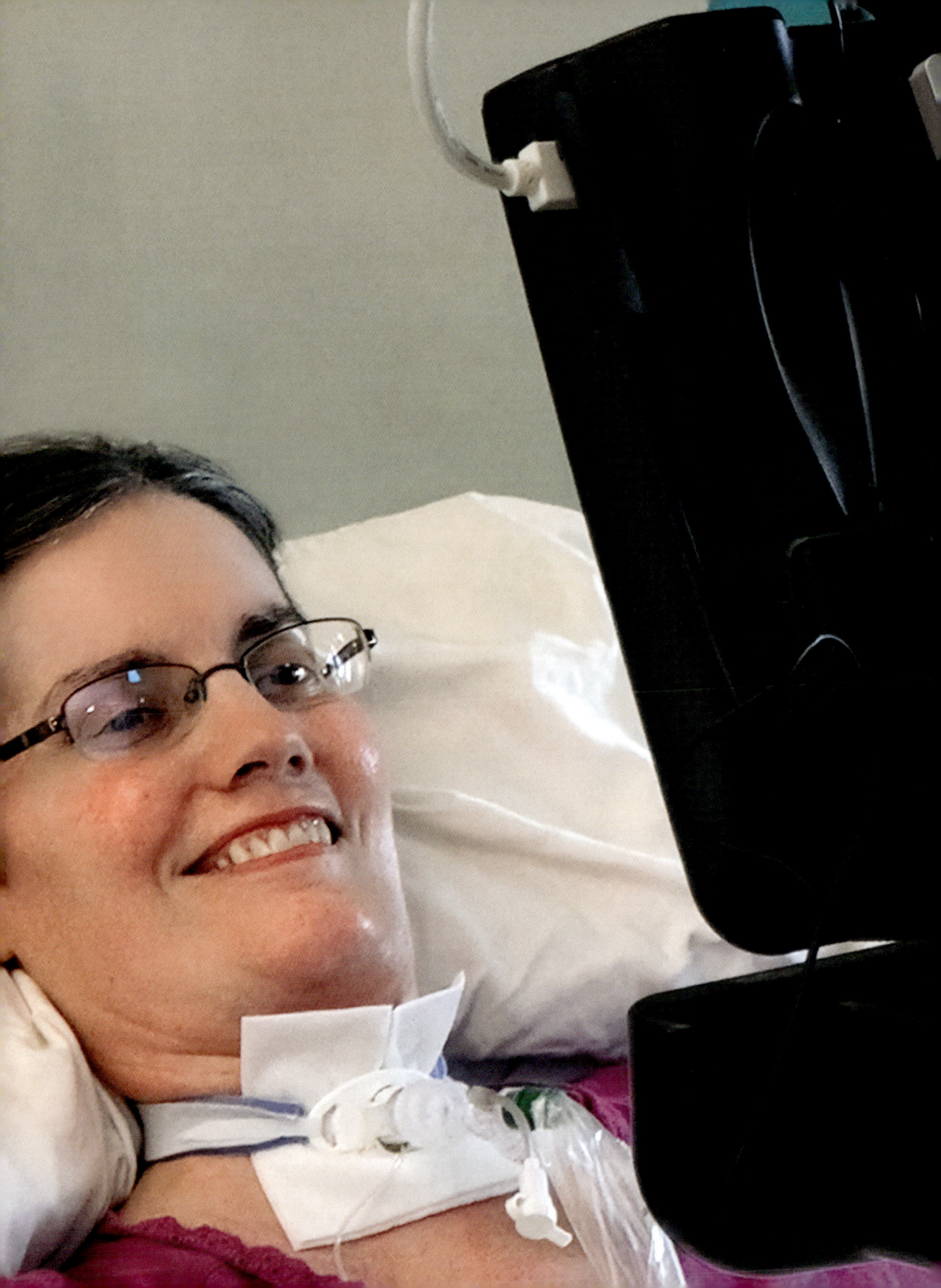

CHAPTER 5

MAKING CONNECTIONS

Scientists are studying ways BCIs can help people communicate. In fact, a small number of people are already using BCIs to write. They choose letters or words on a screen using a cursor controlled by their brain signals. These systems can help people with ALS. This illness, also called Lou Gehrig's disease, attacks nerve cells in the spinal cord and brain. It weakens muscles and can leave people unable to move.

Before BCIs, people with ALS had to use their eye movements to type letters on a screen.

Locked-in syndrome (LIS) is another condition that limits movement. People with LIS are conscious, but they cannot speak or move their muscles. Some cannot even control their eye movements. Communicating is very difficult for them. Researchers are working on systems that respond when users think about moving their hands. People with LIS could use this technology to type or move the cursor on a computer screen.

    New BCI technology could even help people with LIS speak. In one study, electrodes were placed in a speech-related area of a person's brain. These sensors connected to a speech synthesizer. This machine can turn text into sounds that imitate human speech. The person used the BCI to create vowel sounds. Someday, BCIs might allow people with LIS to form whole words and phrases.

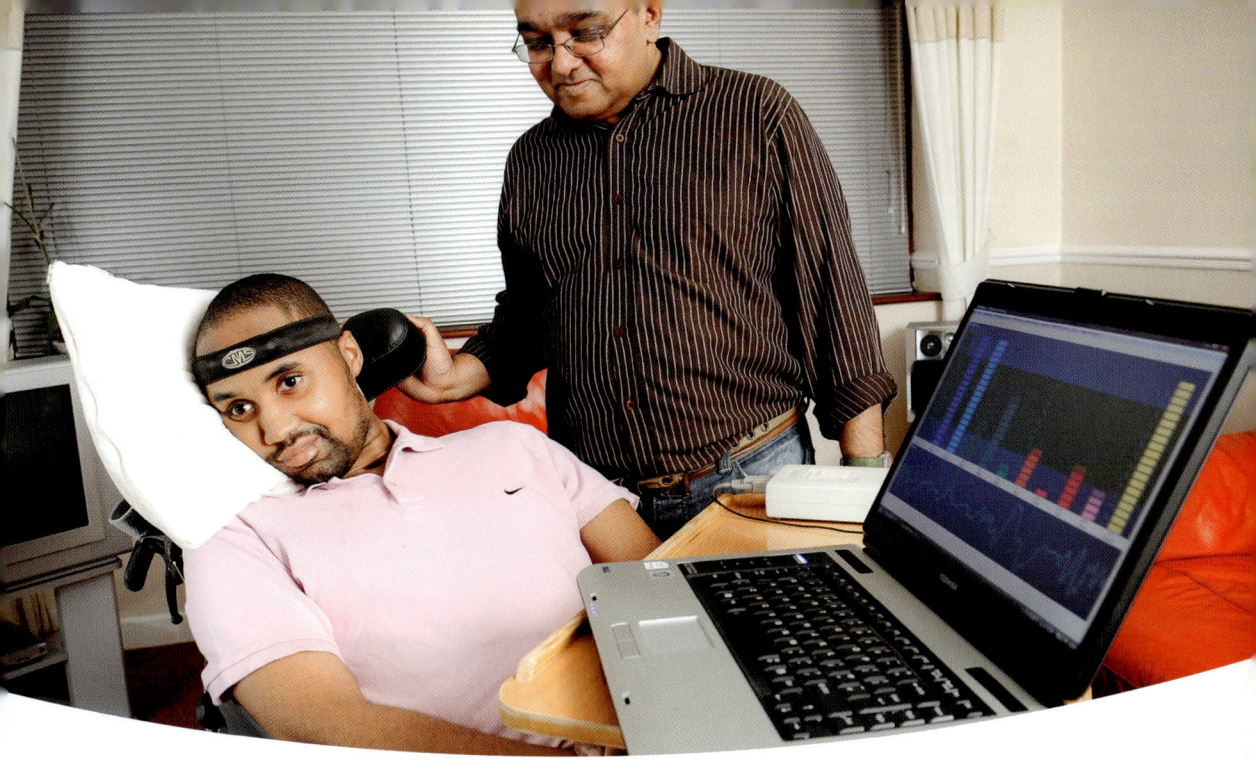

⚠ People with locked-in syndrome can make minimal motions, if any.

Other BCIs help people regain lost senses. In the 1970s, scientists began studying ways BCIs could restore people's sight. In 2017, the FDA approved human trials for one company's system. Users wear special glasses. A video camera in the glasses sends images to a computer. The computer sends instructions back to the glasses, which signal an implant on the person's **retina**.

33

Electrodes in the implant send electrical signals along the optic nerve to the brain. Patients can see light and objects around them.

Cochlear implants help restore hearing. These BCIs have a processor that collects sounds and turns them into signals. The signals are sent to the implant, which transmits them to the auditory nerve. This nerve carries the signals to the brain, where they are interpreted as sounds.

One day, BCIs may help people regain a sense of touch. In 2014, scientists conducted a study with a man who could not use his arms or legs. He could not feel sensation in them, either. Scientists

THINK ABOUT IT

Why would it be important for people with paralysis to regain not just movement but also sensation?

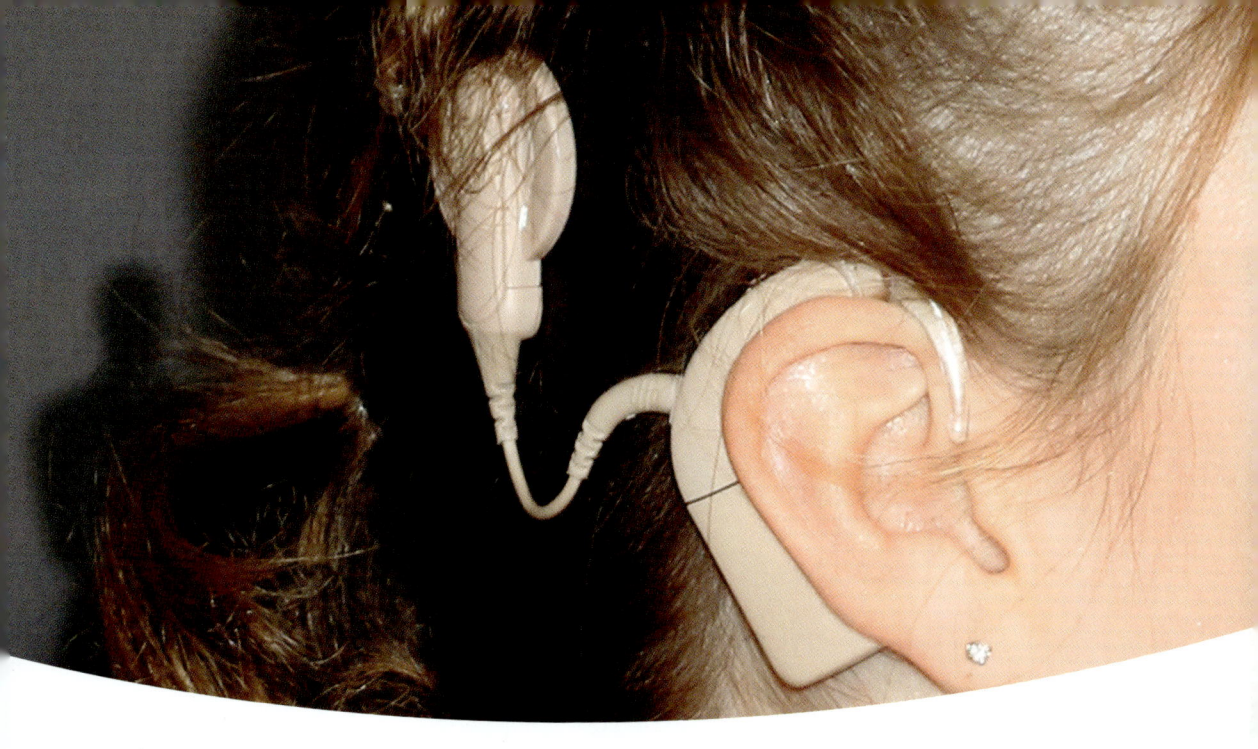

Cochlear implant users wear a device that sits behind the ear. Another part is placed under the skin of the scalp.

placed electrodes in his brain. They connected the electrodes to sensors on a robotic hand. When pressure was applied to the hand, the sensors converted the pressure to electrical signals. These signals stimulated neurons in the man's sensory cortex. He felt like his own fingers were being touched. This successful study shows promise for the future. A sense of touch could give people better control of prosthetic limbs.

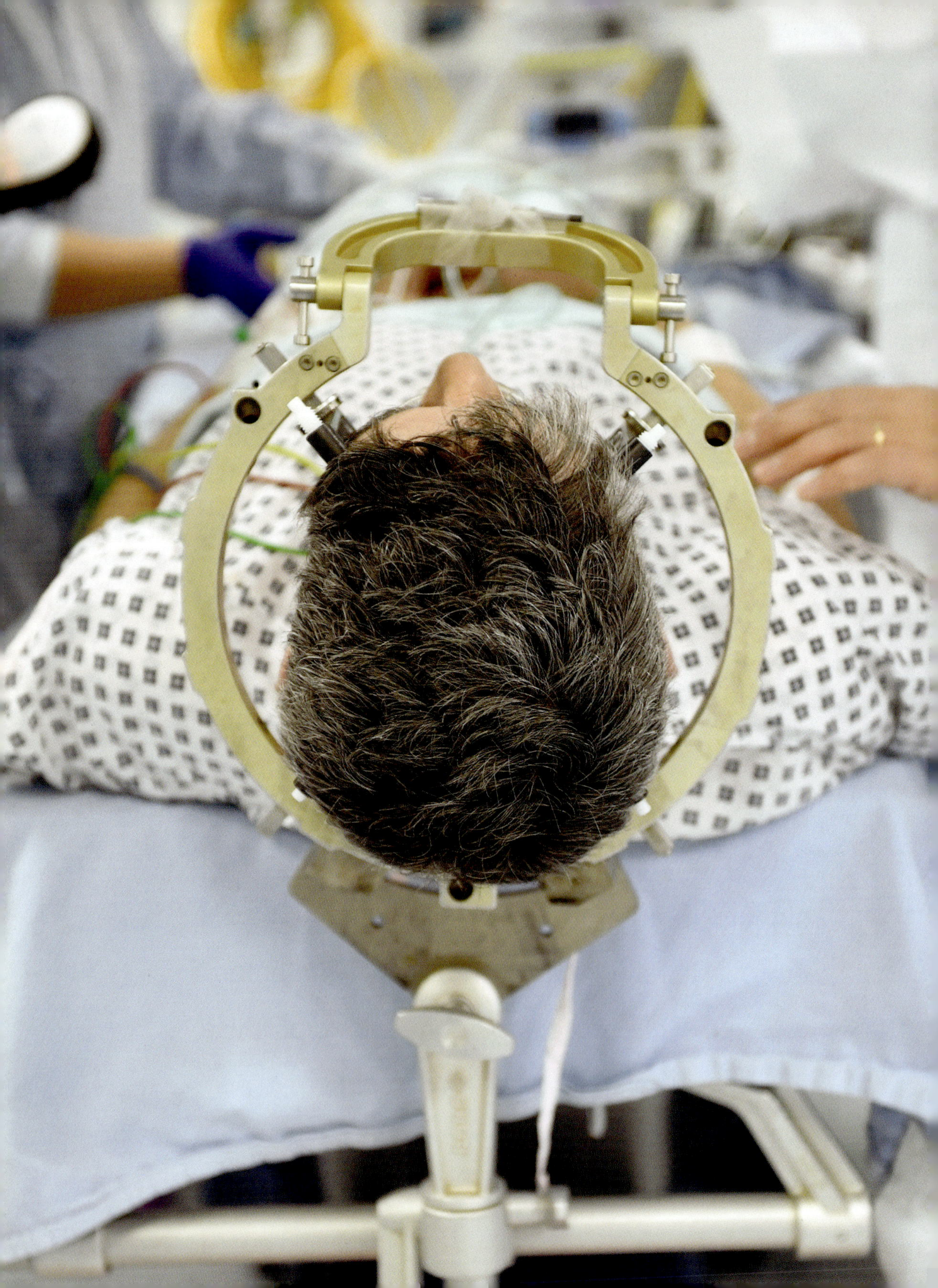

CHAPTER 6

CHALLENGES AHEAD

Scientists have successfully tested many types of BCIs in humans. However, only a few have been approved for long-term use. Before BCIs become common, scientists must overcome several challenges.

Some BCIs use sensors placed directly on a person's brain. Doctors use surgery to implant these sensors. The surgery is often difficult and dangerous. Brain tissue is soft and flexible.

To use deep brain stimulation, doctors must perform surgery.

Surgeons must be very careful. Even so, some brain cells may be damaged.

In addition, BCIs may use electrodes made of hard materials such as metal and glass. These materials can irritate and kill brain cells. And scar tissue tends to grow around the electrodes after they are implanted. This tissue may cut down on the strength of the electrodes' signals.

In some BCI systems, wires pass through the skull and attach to a computer. The wires limit the person's movement. They also increase the risk of infection or bleeding in the brain.

Scientists are working on ways to solve some of these problems. One team is developing a soft, flexible sheet of electrodes made from silicone rubber. This sheet will mimic the dura matter, the **membrane** that covers and protects the brain. It could be permanently placed in the brain.

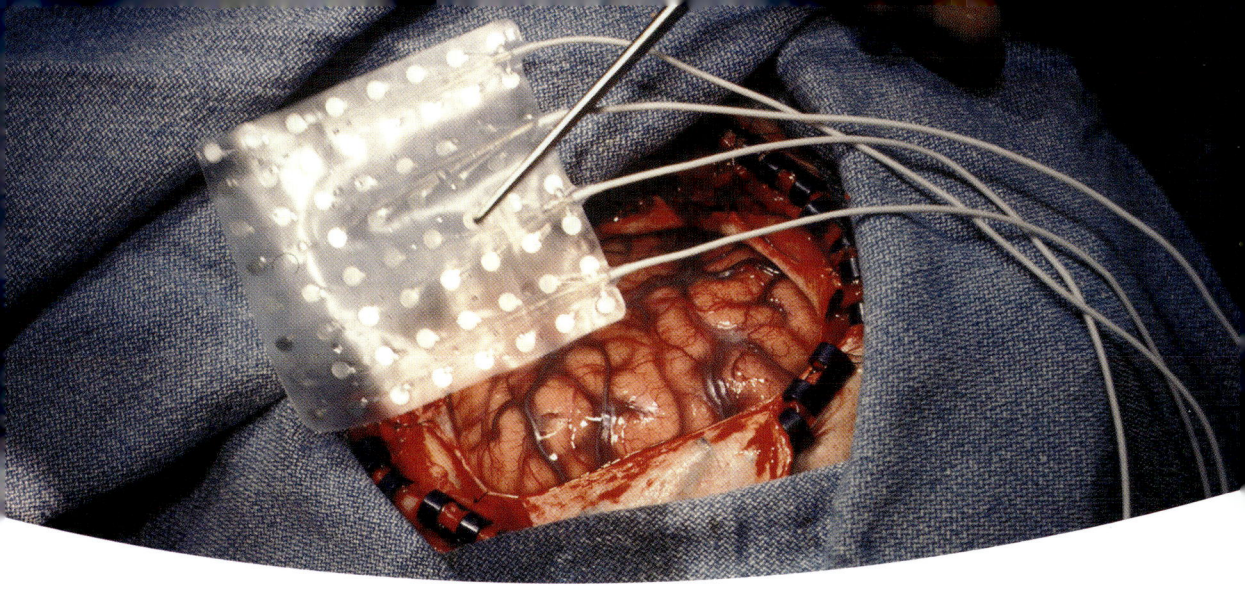

▲ Doctors perform surgery to place a grid of electrodes directly on the brain.

Another research team is testing a stentrode. This device is the size of a paper clip. It contains tiny electrodes that collect signals. A stentrode can be placed directly into a patient's blood vessel. No surgery is needed.

Along with the physical dangers, many BCIs struggle to collect signals in a way that gives users fast and accurate control of a device. Current BCI systems are so slow that they are only useful for people with no other options.

People using P3-based BCIs can only type about five characters per minute. At that rate, writing a single sentence takes several minutes. New types of software are making systems speedier and more reliable.

Using BCIs can cause other problems as well. The training process can be long and difficult. People must learn to use their brains in new ways. They may become frustrated.

Equipment failure could also put people in danger. For instance, suppose someone used a BCI-controlled wheelchair. It could stop working while its user was halfway across a street.

> ## THINK ABOUT IT

Which challenge presented by BCIs do you think will be hardest for scientists to solve? Why?

▲ Doctors are careful to protect each patient's personal information.

One serious concern about BCIs is whether information from the brain could be hacked or stolen. Some people worry that the thoughts of BCI users could be scanned or shared without their permission. Scientists will need to protect against these dangers before BCIs can be used in everyday life.

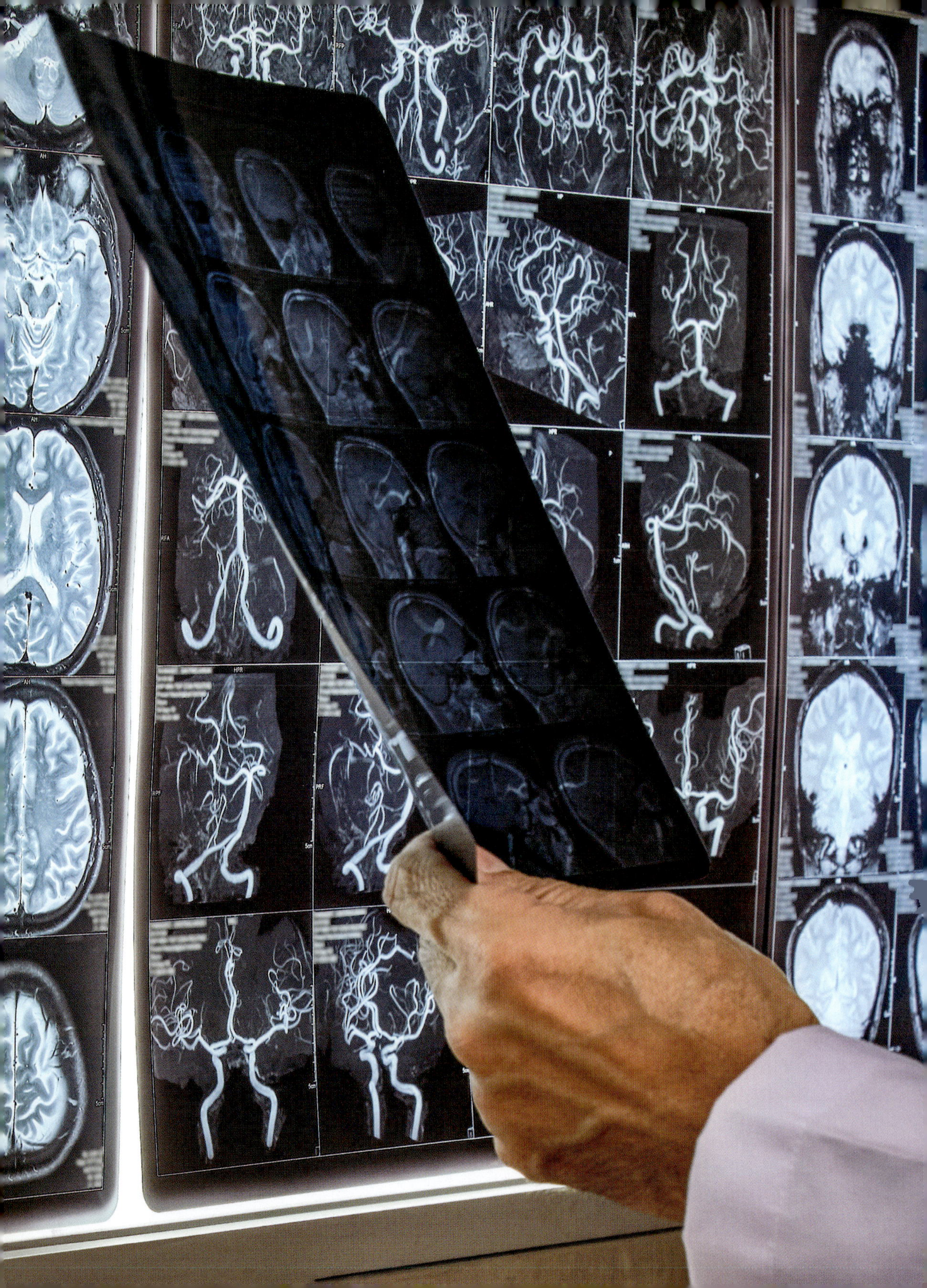

CHAPTER 7

THE FUTURE OF BCIs

Scientists continue to explore the possibilities of what BCIs can do. As BCIs become safer and less expensive, more people may be able to use them. BCI systems could make people smarter, safer, and more focused. For example, many vehicle crashes are caused by distracted or sleepy drivers. A BCI could monitor a driver's attention. It could warn the person before he or she caused an accident.

Scientists still have much to learn about how the human brain works.

BCIs could help people with conditions that affect the nervous system. For instance, BCIs could help monitor and predict seizures. Electrodes under the person's scalp would monitor brain activity. The electrodes would send information to a device implanted in the skull, behind the ear, or in the chest. By tracking this information, a BCI could warn the person when a seizure might occur. That way, the person could get to a safe place before the seizure began.

BCI-based games are also being developed. Some are created to help people. One example is a game for children with attention deficit

THINK ABOUT IT

If our brains merge with machines, are we still human? Or do we become robots?

▲ Some scientists have experimented with BCIs that would allow users to play computer games.

hyperactivity disorder (ADHD). This game is currently being tested. It helps children learn to focus on tasks.

Scientists have even experimented with using BCIs to link human brains. One day, people may be able to link up with others to share thoughts.

FOCUS ON
BRAIN-COMPUTER INTERFACES

Write your answers on a separate piece of paper.

1. Write a paragraph describing one of the things a BCI can help people do.

2. Would you want to try using a BCI? Why or why not?

3. What part of a BCI picks up signals from the user's brain?
    - **A.** the amplifier
    - **B.** the converter
    - **C.** the electrodes

4. How could a BCI help people control prosthetic hands?
    - **A.** It could help them sense when they had a good grip on something they wanted to pick up.
    - **B.** It could help them move the prosthetic hands without thinking.
    - **C.** It could help them send messages to other people with prosthetic limbs.

Answer key on page 48.

GLOSSARY

bionic
Using mechanical parts and electronic devices to help perform tasks.

electrodes
Devices through which electrical signals enter or leave an area.

glands
Organs in the body that produce chemicals used by other parts of the body.

human trial
A study where people volunteer to test a medical treatment to see if it will be safe and effective.

implants
Devices that are placed inside the body using surgery.

membrane
A thin, bendable sheet or skin.

metabolic
Relating to the process used by living things to produce or break down energy.

prosthetic
Having to do with artificial body parts.

retina
The layers of cells at the back of the eye that sense light and send signals to the brain.

seizures
Periods of abnormal electrical activity in the brain and the symptoms (such as shaking or loss of consciousness) they cause.

TO LEARN MORE

BOOKS

Chudler, Eric H. *Brain Lab for Kids: 52 Mind-Blowing Experiments, Models, and Activities to Explore Neuroscience*. Beverly, MA: Quarry Books, 2018.

Mooney, Carla. *The Brain: Journey Through the Universe Inside Your Head*. White River Junction, VT: Nomad Press, 2015.

Swanson, Jennifer. *Brain Games: The Mind-Blowing Science of Your Amazing Brain*. Washington, DC: National Geographic Kids, 2015.

NOTE TO EDUCATORS

Visit **www.focusreaders.com** to find lesson plans, activities, links, and other resources related to this title.

INDEX

amplifier, 18

central nervous system, 15–16

cochlear implants, 11, 34

converter, 18

deep brain stimulation, 20–21

exoskeleton, 26

hearing, 6, 11, 17, 34

locked-in syndrome, 32

motor cortex, 18–19, 25, 28–29

neurons, 6, 10, 15, 28, 35

P3 signals, 11–12, 40

robotic arm, 13, 18, 24–25, 28–29, 35

seizures, 6, 44

sensorimotor rhythms, 12

sight, 7, 33

surgery, 17, 37, 39

Answer Key: 1. Answers will vary; 2. Answers will vary; 3. C; 4. A